A Swimming Pool At The Grand Hotel Oloffson In Port-au-Prince

FACES
AND
PLACES

HAITI

BY ELMA SCHEMENAUER

THE CHILD'S WORLD®, INC.

GRAPHIC DESIGN AND PRODUCTION
Robert E. Bonaker / Graphic Design & Consulting Co.

PHOTO RESEARCH
James R. Rothaus / James R. Rothaus & Associates

COVER PHOTO
Portrait of a Haitian girl
by ©Owen Franken/CORBIS

Library of Congress Cataloging-in-Publication Data
Schemenauer, Elma
Haiti / by Elma Schemenauer.
p. cm.
Includes index.
Summary: Describes Haiti, its history, geography,
people, and customs.
ISBN 1-56766-715-5 (lib. bdg. : alk. paper)

1. Haiti — Juvenile literature.
[1. Haiti.] I. Title.

F1915.2.S34 1999
956.94 — dc21

99-37000
CIP
AC

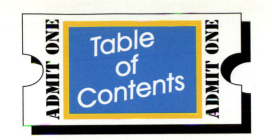

Table of Contents

What if you were in a giant balloon floating high above Earth? You would see huge land areas with water around them. These land areas are called **continents**. Some continents are made up of several countries. Though Haiti is on an island, it is considered part of the North American continent. It is 565 miles southeast of Florida.

Western Hemisphere

Eastern Hemisphere

Both Haiti (white) And U.S.A. (green) Are In The West

Together, Haiti and the Dominican Republic make up the island of *Hispaniola*. The Dominican Republic is east of Haiti. North, west, and south of Haiti are Atlantic Ocean waters. South of Haiti, these waters are often called the Caribbean Sea.

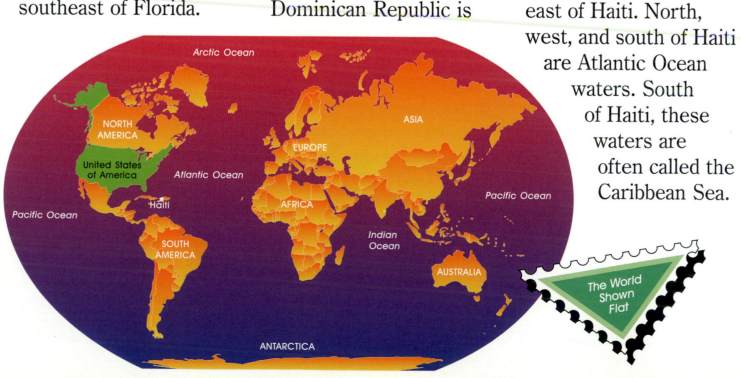

Arctic Ocean

NORTH AMERICA

United States of America

Atlantic Ocean

Pacific Ocean

Haiti

SOUTH AMERICA

AFRICA

EUROPE

ASIA

Indian Ocean

Pacific Ocean

AUSTRALIA

ANTARCTICA

The World Shown Flat

Close-Up of Haiti

UNITED STATES
STATE OF FLORIDA

B A H A M A S

*Atlantic
Ocean*

CUBA

HAITI · DOMINICAN
REPUBLIC

JAMAICA

ISLAND OF HISPANIOLA

PUERTO RICO
U.S. POSSESSION

Caribbean Sea

COLUMBIA   VENEZUELA

A Man And His Donkey On The Road To Lake Saumâtre

TORTUE

Cap Haïtien

GONÂVE

GRANDE CAYEMITE

Lake Saumâtre

Port-au-Prince ★

VACHE

CORBIS/Tony Arruza

Cap Haïtien On Haiti's Atlantic Coast

CORBIS/Adam Woolfitt

Haiti looks like the mouth of a giant crocodile reaching west into the Atlantic Ocean. Flat plains line Haiti's coasts, but about three-quarters of the country is mountainous. The mountain ranges have large plains between them. Most Haitians live on these plains.

Haiti owns several small islands near its coasts. The main ones are Tortue, Gonâve, Grande Cayemite, and Vache.

CORBIS/The Purcell Team

Fields Cover Hillsides In Rural Haiti

There Are Very Few Trees Left In Haiti

CORBIS/Owen Franken

Lush green forests once covered Haiti. Today, few trees are left because a lot of Haiti's beautiful wood was sent to other lands. Also, Haitians cut down many trees to make farmland and much-needed firewood. Haiti does still have a few trees such as orange, lime, mango, and coffee trees, as well as coconut palms. Some forest areas still exist.

The country has no large mammals or poisonous snakes, but it has many lizards. These include **anoles**, which can change color from yellow or brown to green. Fish include barracuda and red snapper.

A Rhinoceros Iguana At A Port-au-Prince Zoo

CORBIS/John Tinning; Frank Lane Picture Agency

Port-au-Prince

CORBIS/Joe McDonald

A Haitian Boa Climbing On A Tree Branch

Slaves
Revolting
Against
French
Colonial
Forces

Port-au-Prince

CORBIS/Bettmann

For many years, *Arawak* Indians farmed on the lush green island of Hispaniola. In 1492, European explorer Christopher Columbus found the island. When Spain, Britain, and France heard about the island, they all wanted it. At last, in 1697, France took control of what is now Haiti. Under French rule it became a rich source of coffee, sugarcane, cocoa, wood, and cotton.

The French brought in African slaves to work the fields. In time, the slaves revolted, led by Toussaint L'Ouverture, Jean-Jacques Dessalines, and others. On January 1, 1804, the former slaves set up their own country, Haiti.

CORBIS/Bettmann

Explorer Christopher Columbus (1451-1506)

But the new country had problems, including poverty and fighting between different groups. In 1915, the American Marines came to try to restore order.

Haiti's First Emperor, Faustin Soutonque, In Council In 1849

CORBIS

Haiti Today

"Papa Doc" Francois Duvalier Stands Behind His Son "Baby Doc" Jean-Claude

When the Americans left in 1934, Haiti still had problems. In 1957, Dr. Francois Duvalier, or "Papa Doc," gained power as president. He was a Haitian himself, but cruel to his people. He had many sent away or killed. "Papa Doc's" son, "Baby Doc," took over after his father, but did not govern much better. In 1986, he fled to France after the Haitians revolted.

Haitians stumbled towards democracy. In 1987, they wrote a new **constitution**. In 1990, they elected Jean-Bertrand Aristide president. Aristide was a Roman Catholic priest who tried to help the poor. Haiti's army soon forced him out.

The Presidential Palace In Port-au-Prince

But in 1994, at the end of Aristide's term as president, the Americans had him returned to power. In 1995, Haiti held another election. Their new constitution said nobody could be president twice in a row, so they could not re-elect Aristide. Instead, they elected René Préval, who had worked with Aristide.

CORBIS/AFP

CORBIS/Tony Arruza

CORBIS/Owen Franken

★ Port-au-Prince

Musicians Play
Bamboo Horns
In A Rowboat
In The Bay
Off Tortue

TORTUE

★ Port-au-Prince

• Jacmel

A Street Vendor In Port-au-Prince

CORBIS/Tony Arruza

In Haiti, most people have an African background. Their ancestors were often people from West Africa. A few Haitians are **mulattoes**. They are lighter-skinned people with a mixed African and European (often French) background.

A Woman Selling Produce At A Market In Jacmel

CORBIS/Kelly-Mooney Photography

Some mulattoes are rich, but most Haitians are among the world's poorest people. Hoping for a better life, many have risked their lives trying to reach the United States by boat. Some of those with a bit more money have moved to France or Canada.

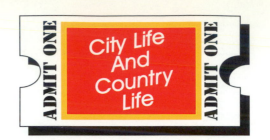

A Thatched Adobe House In The Country

More than two-thirds of Haitians live in the country. They build their houses of sticks and branches covered with plaster or mud. The family usually cooks outdoors, and children may sleep on straw mats on the floor.

CORBIS/Marc Garanger

Houses Made From Old Sheets Of Steel In A "Shantytown" In Port-au-Prince

In cities, poor people live in **shantytowns**. They build houses with pieces of cardboard, wood, and metal—whatever they can find in garbage dumps. Rich city people live in large houses built of stone, concrete, or wood. They often shop in modern stores and eat in fancy hotels and restaurants.

CORBIS/Peter Turnley

★ Port-au-Prince

CORBIS/The Purcell Team

Uniformed Girls In Class In Soleil

Port-au-Prince
Soleil

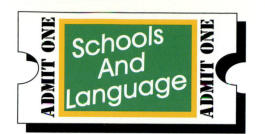

An Election Sign In Port-au-Prince

CORBIS/Paul A. Souders

The government runs some schools in Haiti, but most schools are run by churches. Haitians know that schooling helps children get better jobs when they grow up. But many children get little schooling because they must work to help their families or because the school is too far away. This means a lot of Haitians never learn to read or write.

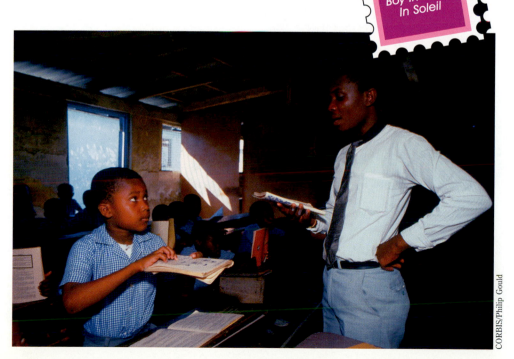

A Teacher Questions A Boy In Class In Soleil

CORBIS/Philip Gould

Creole is one of Haiti's official languages. It is a mix of African languages with French, Spanish, and Portuguese. Almost every Haitian can speak Creole. The country's other official language is French. It is spoken mainly by rich people.

Work

Some Haitians own tiny plots of land, which they farm to try to make a living. They grow crops such as beans, corn, tomatoes, bananas, and sisal (used to make rope). Some raise livestock, including chickens and pigs. Some work for richer people on bigger plots of land, tending crops such as rice, coffee, cocoa, and cotton.

Fishermen Hauling In A Net On The Caribbean Sea In Jacmel

CORBIS/Richard Bickel

A Boy Selling Seashells From A Dugout Canoe Near Port-au-Prince

CORBIS/Richard Bickel

In cities, especially Port-au-Prince, some Haitians work in factories owned by people from the United States, Canada, Japan, or other countries. The Haitians put together pieces sent from these other countries to make toys, clothes, boots, shoes, medical supplies, and other goods.

CORBIS/Archivo Iconografico, S.A.

Port-au-Prince

Jacmel

A Man
Harvesting
Sugarcane

Restaurant Tables At The Grand Hotel Oloffson In Port-au-Prince

★ Port-au-Prince

Haiti's national dish is rice with beans and chicken (when people can get chicken). Haitians also like stews and hot spicy sauces. Among other foods are avocados, wild greens from the fields, oranges, mangoes, millet (a grain), and sorghum (something like corn).

A Woman Chewing On A Piece Of Sugarcane In Port-au-Prince

CORBIS/Paul A. Souders

A Woman Cooking Over A Fire In Rural Haiti

Haitians seldom eat meat. It costs too much. Even families who raise chickens, pigs, or goats may not eat much meat. They need the money they make by selling the eggs, milk, and meat from these animals.

CORBIS/Philip Gould

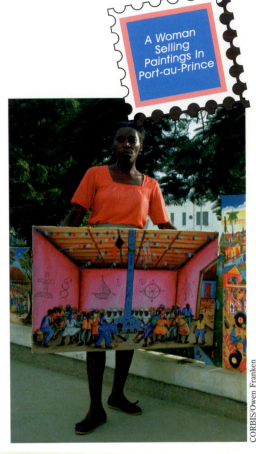

A Woman Selling Paintings In Port-au-Prince

CORBIS/Owen Franken

Haitians love music, singing, and dancing. They play bamboo trumpets and conch-shell horns. Some have real drums, and some use plastic pails as drums. They use dried gourds to make *maracas* (like rattles), too. Much of Haitians' music links them to the past, especially to their ancestors in Africa.

Haitian artists are famous around the world. Their paintings often show Bible stories, African jungles, market scenes, or festivals. In the past, Haitian sculptors worked with wood. Now, since wood is hard to get, they work with flattened steel drums or whatever they can find.

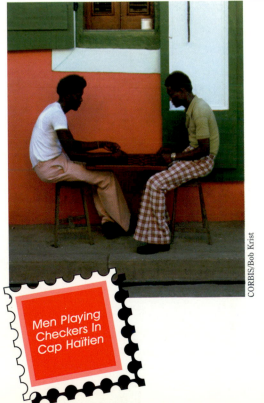

Men Playing Checkers In Cap Haïtien

CORBIS/Bob Krist

In Haiti, New Year's and Independence Day are both the same day— January 1. Other holidays include Ancestors' Day on January 2 and United Nations Day on October 24. Most Haitians are Roman Catholics, so they also celebrate Christian holidays such as All Saints' Day on November 1 and Christmas on December 25.

No matter what they're doing, no matter how poor they are, Haitians can always joke and laugh. Their sense of humor has helped carry them through many hard times. Along with people around the world, they hope better times lie ahead.

Cap Haïtien

Port-au-Prince

CORBIS/Paul A. Sounders

A Father
And Son Relax
On A Beach On
The Southern
Coast

Area
Almost 11,000 square miles (28,000 square kilometers)—about the same size as Maryland.

Population
About 7 million people.

Capital City
Port-au-Prince.

Other Important Cities and Towns
Les Cayes, Gonaïtien, Cap Haïtien, and Pétionville.

Money
The gourde. A gourde is divided into 100 centimes.

National Flag
The flag has two sideways stripes, blue and red. In the center of the flag is the national coat of arms, which has palms on it.

National Song
"La Dessalienne," or "The Song of Dessalines." It begins, "For the country, for the ancestors, let us march united. . . ."

National Holiday
Independence Day on January 1.

Head of Government
The president of Haiti.

National Dance
The *méringue,* also called the wooden leg dance.

A Carnival Performer In Port-au-Prince

Did You Know?

When the former slaves set up their own country in 1804, they gave it its old Arawak name, Haiti, which means "high ground" or "mountainous country."

Haiti was the world's first black **republic.** People in a republic vote for leaders to run a government headed by a president. The United States is a republic, too.

Some Haitian farm families use their pigs like money in a bank. If a child goes to school, they sell a pig to buy a school uniform and books. If someone dies, they sell a pig to pay for the funeral.

Lately people have been planting fast-growing trees in Haiti. These trees help keep the soil from blowing or washing away, as it does when there are no trees to shelter it and hold it together.

How Do You Say?

	HAITIAN CREOLE	HOW TO SAY IT
Hello	bon jou	bawn–hi–hoo
Good-bye	orévwa	aw–ray–vway
Please	souple	soo–pleh
Thank You	mèsi	meh–see
One	youn	yoon
Two	de	deh
Three	twa	twah
Haiti	ayiti	ayee–tee

anoles (uh–NOH–leez)
Anoles are small lizards that can change color. Anoles are found in many country areas of Haiti.

constitution (kon–stih–TOO–shun)
A constitution is a set of laws for a country that state how a country's government is organized. Haiti has a constitution.

continents (KON–tih–nents)
Earth's land areas are divided up into huge sections called continents. Haiti is part of the North American continent.

Creole (KREE–ohl)
Creole is one of Haiti's official languages. It is a mix of African languages with French, Spanish, and Portuguese.

mulattoes (moo–LAH–tohz)
Mulattoes are people who have mixed backgrounds such as African and European. Some Haitians are mulattoes.

republic (ree–PUH–blik)
A republic is a government in which the people have the right to vote. Haiti is a republic.

shantytowns (SHAN–tee–townz)
Shantytowns are poor areas of cities where people live in homes built of cardboard or other materials.

Index

Web Sites

Learn more about Haiti:
http://www.medalia.net/Hhistory.html
http://www.emulateme.com/haiti.htm

Learn about "Papa Doc" Duvalier:
http://www.optonline.com/comptons/ceo/01423_A.html

Read the words to the national anthem of Haiti:
http://www.monumental.com/embassy/hymnnatl.htm

Learn more about Hispaniola:
http://caribbeansupersite.com/hisp/index.htm